THE BOOK
OF
IDENTITY

James John Alayo

All rights reserved. The total or partial reproduction of this work is not allowed, nor its incorporation into a computer system, or its transmission in any form or by any means (electronic, mechanical, photocopying, recording, or otherwise) without the prior written permission of the copyright holder is a violation of these rights and may constitute a crime against intellectual property

The content of this work is the responsibility of the author and does not necessarily reflect the views of the publishing house. All texts and images were provided by the author, who is solely responsible for their rights.

"The Scripture quotations in this publication are from the King James Version. The KJV is public domain in the United States."

Published by Ibukku, LLC
www.ibukku.com
Cover Design: Ángel Flores Guerra Bistrain
Graphic Design: Diana Patricia González Juárez
Copyright © 2024 James John Alayo
ISBN Paperback: 978-1-68574-914-9
ISBN Hardcover: 978-1-68574-916-3
ISBN eBook: 978-1-68574-915-6

Table of Content

Introduction   5

Chapter 1
Identity is given by the Holy Spirit   7

Chapter 2
Searching for our identity   15

Chapter 3
You were created to have your own identity   27

Chapter 4
Three types of identity   33

Chapter 5
Human identity and God's Identity   43

Chapter 6
Internal and external identity   53

Chapter 7
Our personality is not our identity   61

Chapter 8
In a new identity comes something new from God   69

Chapter 9
Losing to Gain   77

Chapter 10
The Adversary doesn't want you to have identity   85

Chapter 11
Our identity is a Grace from God   93

Introduction

Every genuine Christian must have a genuine and unique identity, and that unique and genuine identity will not be obtained by doing what other Christians do or by wanting to resemble other Christians. That identity will be obtained because it is the Holy Spirit who will give it.

The identity that each Christian has is given by God, and God will use His Word and His Spirit to give it.

For this reason, every man or woman of God was different from one another, not only because of the difference in their calling but also because each of them had a different purpose and identity in their calling.

Every genuine Christian must seek their own identity, and that identity will only be given by God through His Spirit.

Chapter 1
Identity is given by the Holy Spirit

Every genuine Christian will have their own identity. This identity will not be obtained by doing what other Christians do or by wanting to resemble others; this identity will be obtained because it will be given by the Holy Spirit.

The identity that every genuine Christian must have has to be given by God and His Spirit.

For this reason, every man or woman of God was different from one another, not only because of their calling but also because each one had a different identity.

Every Christian must seek their own and unique identity, which will be given by God through His Holy Spirit and His Word.

What is identity?

Identity comprises the qualities, traits, aptitudes, or characteristics of a person that distinguish them from others. In the Bible, we can see some examples of identity:

"*3. But the angel of the Lord said to Elijah the Tishbite, Arise, go up to meet the messengers of the king of Samaria, and say unto them, Is it not because there is not a God in Israel, that ye go to enquire of Baalzebub the god of Ekron? 4. Now therefore thus saith the Lord, Thou shalt not come down from that bed on which thou art gone up, but shalt surely die. And Elijah departed. 5. And when the messengers turned back unto him, he said unto them, Why are ye now turned back? 6. And they said unto him, There came a man up to meet us, and said unto us, Go, turn again unto the king that sent you, and say unto him, Thus saith the Lord, Is it not because there is not a God in Israel, that thou sendest to enquire of Baalzebub the god of Ekron? therefore thou shalt not come down from that bed on which thou art gone up, but shalt surely die. 7. And he said unto them, What manner of man was he which came up to meet you, and told you these words? 8. And they answered him, He was an hairy man, and girt with a girdle of leather about his loins. And he said, It is Elijah the Tishbite."*
2 Kings 1:3-8

King Ocozias recognized that it was Elias who had encountered his messengers because of the prophet Elias's characteristics, such as his clothing, hair, etc. A person of that era did not dress the way Elias did, nor did they speak with the certainty and clarity that Elias spoke. His manner of dress and expression were unique to the prophet Elias; that was his identity.

The prophet Elias, before being called by God, was probably like the other people where he lived. Likely, his clothing, way of speaking, and words were like those of his people. However, when God called him to be a prophet, He gave him a different identity, a unique identity. No one was like Elias. Now he was a prophet, and God gave him a new identity. He would now be known as the prophet Elias.

Let's look at the example of the prophet Eliseo:

"19. So he departed thence, and found Elisha the son of Shaphat, who was plowing with twelve yoke of oxen before him, and he with the twelfth: and Elijah passed by him, and cast his mantle upon him. 20. And he left the oxen, and ran after Elijah, and said, Let me, I pray thee, kiss my father and my mother, and then I will follow thee. And he said unto him, Go back again: for what have I done to thee? 21. And he returned back from him, and took a yoke of oxen, and slew them, and boiled their flesh with the instruments of the oxen, and gave unto the people, and they did eat. Then he arose, and went after Elijah, and ministered unto him."
1 Kings 19:19-21

In this case, we can see that Eliseo was a man working in the field, but when the prophet Elias, guided by God and His Spirit, called Eliseo, he left everything he had and followed Elias. Why? Because Eliseo would be the next prophet. Who would take Elias's place? Eliseo would now begin to be shaped by the Holy Spirit to be the next prophet and Elias's successor. Just as Elias had his own identity as a prophet of God, so too would Eliseo, formed and aided by the Holy Spirit of God, have his own identity.

Every Christian is unique

Every Christian must have and needs to have their own identity. Just like the prophet Elias and the prophet Eliseo, you and I need to be molded by the Holy Spirit of God to have our own identity.

When a Christian does not have their own identity, they may desire to resemble other Christians and will want to imitate the ways or attitudes of another person.

This lack of identity in a Christian may be due to the need for that person to be molded and shaped by the Holy Spirit so that the Holy Spirit can form in them the identity that God wants to give them.

A Christian who lacks identity and does not seek it in God will seek it outside of Him and outside of His will. Since they do not have their own identity as a son or daughter of God, they will want to resemble, will want to be what they believe they should be, but not because that is the will of God, but because the person, by their own will, wants and chooses how to be.

To have the identity that God, through His Holy Spirit, wants to give us, it is necessary to enter into God's process, to be in dealings with God, and to remain and go through that process correctly.

Only then can we be formed and have God's identity for our lives.

"1. And I, brethren, could not speak unto you as unto spiritual, but as unto carnal, even as unto babes in Christ. 2. I have fed you with milk, and not with meat: for hitherto ye were not able to bear it, neither yet now are ye able. 3. For ye are yet carnal: for whereas there is among you envying, and strife, and divisions, are ye not carnal, and walk as men? 4. For while one saith, I am of Paul; and another, I am of Apollos; are ye not carnal? 5. Who then is Paul, and who is Apollos, but ministers by whom ye believed, even as the Lord gave to every man?"
1 Corinthians 3:1-5

In this scripture, we can see that there were quarrels and disagreements among the brothers and sisters in Corinth. Some said, "I am of Paul," and others, "I am of Apollos." These brothers and sisters were taking on an identity, either that of Paul or Apollos, to identify with that name and be known as part of one of them.

Paul and Apollos were men of God with an identity given to them by the Holy Spirit.

When a Christian knows their identity as a child of God, they will not identify with a name or something similar, but they will identify as the Apostle Paul or Apollos did; they will identify with what God has given them, and they will be known for who they are in Christ Jesus. They will know their position in the body of Christ, and knowing all this, they will not need to take something from others for themselves because God has already given them what is theirs, their own genuine and unique identity.

"And I, brethren, could not speak unto you as unto spiritual, but as unto carnal, even as unto babes in Christ."
1 Corinthians 3:1

The Apostle Paul tells these brothers and sisters that they are immature, like children, because they did not yet have their own identity and needed to take the name of someone who had their own identity and cling to that name.

They still needed to be molded and shaped by the Holy Spirit to have their own identity.

Similarly, if you or I do not have an identity that comes from God, given by His Holy Spirit, we will seek it outside of Him, and that mold, that example we will have, will not be from God but human. By taking the identity of other brothers and sisters in the faith, we will never become what God wants us to be.

Each child of God, each Christian, is unique and has their own identity.

The Scriptures tell us in the Gospel of John about the declaration of John the Baptist:

"John answered and said, A man can receive nothing, except it be given him from heaven."
John 3:27

The identity of a genuine Christian comes from above, from heaven.

When we want to be like other Christians, we are desiring to have what God gave to that person. But just as God gave that Christian their own identity, God has a unique and personal identity for you and me.

If we want to imitate the identity of another Christian, we may never know what our own identity is. By copying someone else, we blind ourselves and cannot see or understand the identity that God wants to give us.

Many Christians are trapped in the identity of another person and cannot discover what God has for them because they think that is their identity and believe they have already found it.

For example, in the world, when a person wants to look like someone else physically, they imitate their way of dressing and might even change their body through surgery to achieve an external resemblance. However, inside, this person is very different from the one they are trying to imitate.

There is a human identity that every human being has, but upon knowing God, we need to be shaped and molded to obtain the identity that God wants us to have, and only the Holy Spirit of God can give us that identity.

Identity in a Christian is given by God, by His Spirit.

Chapter 2
Searching for our identity

When a baby arrives in this world, they go through a growth process and must pass through it. This process of growth and development consists of two areas:

1. Physical area (external)
2. Mental area (internal)

In the physical area, the child will go through different processes and stages of growth, and their body will undergo many changes until it reaches full development. According to their age, their body will change, and their physical characteristics will be in constant flux until they mature completely.

In the mental area, it will be similar. As a young child, they will want to play and explore a lot, without responsibilities or worries. They will feel free and very spontaneous. However, as they grow and change, they will start to think differently, gain more responsibilities, and later, when they are a youth or an adult, their thoughts should be clearer and better equipped to make decisions.

But not every human being, after going through those physical and mental processes, will become what they should be at the age they should be. Some people will not fully mature in their intellect or mentality. This can happen for many reasons, which is why not all humans have the same IQ, intelligence, or mental capacity.

Similarly, in the physical area, some people are born with physical deficiencies, while others may experience accidents or illnesses during their lives that cause their bodies to no longer be the same as before the accident or illness.

This also happens to Christians.

When a Christian is born again, in the gospel, they must go through a process with the Holy Spirit, in which the Holy Spirit will work with this newly born person to give them a new identity.

Many Christians need to be healed and repaired internally, in our minds and feelings. God will work with each of us in the way and in the area we need.

Just as in the world when a child is born, there is a process of internal and external changes during their growth, the same happens in the life of a Christian when they convert to Christ Jesus. A process of change and spiritual growth will begin, and it will be the Holy Spirit of God who will work with this person in the necessary areas.

Some people will need to change more in one area, while other Christians will need to change more in other areas of their life and personality.

In the world, people seek an identity, and that identity is earthly, of this world, aligned with the prince of this world.

"3. But if our gospel be hid, it is hid to them that are lost: 4. In whom the god of this world hath blinded the minds of them which believe not, lest the light of the glorious gospel of Christ, who is the image of God, should shine unto them."
2 Corinthians 4:3-4

Christians must seek their own identity with the help of God, through His Word and His Holy Spirit.

"For we are his workmanship, created in Christ Jesus unto good works, which God hath before ordained that we should walk in them."
Ephesians 2:10

"But the anointing which ye have received of him abideth in you, and ye need not that any man teach you: but as the same anointing teacheth you of all things, and is truth, and is no lie, and even as it hath taught you, ye shall abide in him."
1 John 2:27

Every genuine Christian will be born again by the Spirit of God (John 3:1-10). After this new birth, they will go through a process of spiritual development and growth, and during this process, this man or woman, this Christian, will need to seek their own identity.

Some Christians will discover this identity faster than others, while others will take longer. This will depend on their dedication to God and their communion with Him through His Word and His Spirit.

Let's see what the Scriptures tell us:

"11. Of whom we have many things to say, and hard to be uttered, seeing ye are dull of hearing. 12. For when for the time ye ought to be teachers, ye have need that one teach you again which be the first principles of the oracles of God; and are become such as have need of milk, and not of strong meat. 13. For every one that useth milk is unskilful in the word of righteousness: for he is a babe. 14. But strong meat belongeth to them that are of full age, even those who by reason of use have their senses exercised to discern both good and evil."
Hebrews 5:11-14

The writer, inspired by the Spirit of God, exhorts the church and points out that although many (those who have been called) should already be teachers, they are not yet. This implies that many of these brothers and sisters were still in a process of learning and spiritual growth and had not yet become what they were called to be.

Many children of God, Christians, even after many years, are still searching for their identity. They should already have an identity as children of God in the body of Christ, but due to their lack of communion with God through His Word and Spirit, or because they have not fully surrendered to God, they are still on the path and have not yet grown spiritually in many areas of their lives, including their identity as children of God.

As Christians, we must have an identity, and that identity will be given to us by God. God will use His Word and His Holy Spirit, and He will use life situations or revelations to give us that identity.

When Jesus came into this world, He had a very defined identity. He knew who He was, the reason He had come to this world, His purpose, and His mission.

"36. Jesus answered, My kingdom is not of this world: if my kingdom were of this world, then would my servants fight, that I should not be delivered to the Jews: but now is my kingdom not from hence. 37. Pilate therefore said unto him, Art thou a king then? Jesus answered, Thou sayest that I am a king. To this end was I born, and for this cause came I into the world, that I should bear witness unto the truth. Every one that is of the truth heareth my voice."
John 18:36-37

What happens if we do not seek our own identity in God?

When a Christian does not seek their identity with God's help to discover their mission and purpose, they risk searching for their identity in the same way as people who do not know God. These people look at what others do, observe how they are, and copy that or do something similar.

God can call someone with a specific purpose and plan, but if the person called does not know God's purpose for their life, they will do what others do or end up frustrated by not knowing what to do as a child of God and not knowing God's purpose for their life.

> *"13. Then certain of the vagabond Jews, exorcists, took upon them to call over them which had evil spirits the name of the Lord Jesus, saying, We adjure you by Jesus whom Paul preacheth. 14. And there were seven sons of one Sceva, a Jew, and chief of the priests, which did so. 15. And the evil spirit answered and said, Jesus I know, and Paul I know; but who are ye? 16. And the man in whom the evil spirit was leaped on them, and overcame them, and prevailed against them, so that they fled out of that house naked and wounded."*
> Acts 19:13-16

Clearly, these Jewish men were not directed by God to perform that action. They wanted to do what the apostle Paul or the Lord Jesus did; and when they tried to do it, it did not go well because the Holy Spirit did not support them with His power to carry out that action.

Many Christians do or want to do what they see other Christians doing, and that is because they still do not have their own identity.

In Christianity, each believer has an individual and unique identity given by the Holy Spirit.

"For we are his workmanship, created in Christ Jesus unto good works, which God hath before ordained that we should walk in them."
Ephesians 2:10

The works that a Christian does, like those done by the apostle Paul or the prophets of the Old Testament, were part of their identity. In the same way, the works that each Christian does are part of their identity.

What we do as children of God is something that God has prepared for each child individually.

For this reason, the sons of Sceva (Acts 19:13-16) could not free the demon-possessed man because they were not called to do that; it was not part of their identities. They were trying to do something that was not granted to them. Those works were part of the identity of the apostle Paul or the Lord Jesus, and when they tried to copy them, the work they attempted did not go well.

Every genuine Christian has different gifts or ministries, given according to the will of the Holy Spirit (1 Corinthians 12), and this will be in accordance with the eternal purpose that God has for each one. This gift or ministry is a part of a Christian's identity. This is why we see in the Bible that the apostles of Jesus or the prophets of the Old Testament each had different gifts or ministries, and each individually performed different signs.

What each one did was unique to their calling and purpose, and that was part of their own identity.

When we do not seek our identity as children of God, we will do things or want to perform signs that have not been given or distributed to us by the Holy Spirit.

If a person was called to be an evangelist or a pastor, but does not know what God has called them to do, and does not understand God's plan and purpose for their life, this person may end up doing other works for which God has not called them.

When we do not have communion with the Holy Spirit, when we do not read and meditate on the Word of God, when we do not practice it, we will be separated from God and His will, and we will be Christians lacking identity.

On God's path, there are different stages

When a child is born, they have certain habits and attitudes. As they grow, they will develop different attitudes, ways of thinking, and ways of doing things. This is part of their growth, part of their physical and emotional development.

Similarly, when a Christian is born again, they have certain attitudes. As they grow, their perspective on the Christian life changes; they become more mature. If this Christian person has been in constant communion with God through His Word and His Spirit, they will grow spiritually much more.

Later, when they are more mature, they will know and understand much more about Christianity.

God may call someone to be a preacher, prophet, or teacher, or He may call someone to have a specific ministry, such as a pastor. He may also give them a spiritual gift (1 Corinthians 12). But when God calls this Christian to a ministry, such as a pastor, they will have that identity at that stage of their life. However, God may later call them to another ministry in addition to the one they already had; for example, to be a prophet (and also give them the anointing of a prophet). With this new calling, this man called by God will now identify not only as a pastor but also as a prophet.

When God called me to preach His word, He never revealed to me that a few years later I would have another ministry. At the beginning, He simply told me to "preach," and He communicated this to me in many ways. So I began to do what He told me: preach. For more than 12 years, I preached wherever God led me. I was an evangelist and identified as an evangelist, and everyone who knew me knew me as the evangelist James.

After 12 years, God began to use me in prophecies, and my prophetic calling started to develop. After some more time, God called me and spoke to me to become a pastor.

In each stage of each calling that God gave me, I identified with that calling, and that was my identity. When I was an evangelist, I identified as an evangelist; that was my identity. Later, when God used me prophetically, I no longer identified solely as an evangelist but also with my prophetic calling. My identity, in addition to being an evangelist, also included that prophetic line, and those ministries started to blend within me. Then, when God called and confirmed me as a pastor, my identity aligned with and joined this new direction from God for my life.

God can call someone to be an evangelist, and later, in the future, He can call this same person to be a prophet. However, if this person does not have communion with God through His Word and His Spirit, they might think and believe that they are only an evangelist and not a prophet. They might even limit themselves and the prophetic calling they have, not developing it properly due to a lack of communion with the Holy Spirit and the Word of God.

In Christianity, there are stages. Just as in the natural world a baby, a child, and a young person are different, and each stage of their lives and growth has different qualities that identify them according to their age, so too in our spiritual growth there are stages. In each stage of our Christian life, God can give us a gift or a ministry, and we can characterize ourselves with it, identify with it, and be known for it.

For example, a baby cannot be known or have the identity of a child, and a child neither has nor should have the identity of a young person or a baby, unless something is wrong with them or they have not been able to develop correctly due to some circumstance.

Let's look at a scripture:

"12. For when for the time ye ought to be teachers, ye have need that one teach you again which be the first principles of the oracles of God; and are become such as have need of milk, and not of strong meat. 13. For every one that useth milk is unskilful in the word of righteousness: for he is a babe. 14. But strong meat belongeth to them that are of full age, even those who by reason of use have their senses exercised to discern both good and evil."
Hebrews 5:12-14

If we are not in communion with God through His Word and His Spirit, we will not grow correctly. However, if we are in constant communion with the Spirit of God and His Word, we will grow correctly and find our identity.

"When I was a child, I spake as a child, I understood as a child, I thought as a child: but when I became a man, I put away childish things."
1 Corinthians 13:11

It is the Spirit of God who will work with us to give us our identity.

If we are close to God, we will be what He wants us to be, we will know what He wants us to know, and we will do what He wants us to do.

It is very important that every genuine Christian seeks their identity because the identity that God wants us to have is what He truly wants us to be. If we do not seek and do not have a genuine identity from God, we will be incomplete.
Seek your identity in God.

Chapter 3
You were created to have your own identity

Each child of God was individually created to have their own identity.

Before becoming followers of Christ, when we were in the world, we were known for being a certain way; that was our identity. Some of us were known for being drinkers of wine or liquor, others possibly for liking to argue or fight, etc.

That was who some of us were when we were in the world, that was our identity, our introduction. But when we came to God's path, by His sovereign and great mercy, He changed us to give us a new identity.

This identity is not like that of the world, nor is it like that of other children of God. It is a unique identity that God gives to each of His children, and this identity that He gives us will align with His purpose for our lives.

"And we know that all things work together for good to them that love God, to them who are the called according to his purpose."
Romans 8:28

Our identity as children of God is not based on other Christians. In other words, the foundation of our identity cannot and should not be based on doing what other Christians do. The foundation of our identity must be based on Jesus Christ, in our desire to be as He wants us to be, and we will achieve this through His Word, by His Spirit, in our communion and relationship with God.

The new identity that every genuine Christian will have is founded and based on the Word of God and the help, revelation, and guidance of the Holy Spirit.

"For we are his workmanship, created in Christ Jesus unto good works, which God hath before ordained that we should walk in them."
Ephesians 2:10

Let's look at the example of Jesus, the Messiah:

In the book of Isaiah, chapter 53, the Bible tells us that the Messiah was to come into the world. Throughout this chapter, many characteristics of the Messiah's life, purpose, and life on Earth are revealed. This was the identity of the Christ, the Messiah who was to come to Earth. Many who recognized that Jesus was the Messiah knew it was Him because this written prophecy was fulfilled in Him, including all the qualities described in that prophecy. Furthermore, Jesus declared why He had come to this world and what His purpose was.

This was the identity of Jesus, the Messiah, while He was in the flesh in this world.

No one else could do what Jesus did because those signs were reserved exclusively for the Messiah. Those signs would identify Him as the Messiah. They were unique to Him and part of His identity.

Likewise, each of us was created to be unique, and we were created for a mission and a purpose. But if we do not know why we have been created and called, we will have an identity, but it will be an incomplete identity because we will lack knowledge of it and feel compelled to do or imitate what others do.

If Jesus, the Christ, the Messiah, did not have an identity, what would have happened? Would He have had to do what the other religious leaders of His time did? Would He have had to be and conduct His ministry like others did in His time?

This is what many followers of Christ who do not yet have an identity do—they watch and imitate what others do.

Let's look at another example of a unique identity:

"1. In those days came John the Baptist, preaching in the wilderness of Judaea, 2. And saying, Repent ye: for the kingdom of heaven is at hand. 3. For this is he that was spoken of by the prophet Esaias, saying, The voice of one crying in the wilderness, Prepare ye the way of the Lord, make his paths straight. 4. And the same John had his raiment of camel's hair, and a leathern girdle about his loins; and his meat was locusts and wild honey."
Matthew 3:1-4

The prophet John the Baptist was sent by God to baptize (John 1:33), but the Bible does not record any healings or miracles performed by him. We can also see that he had a very unique way of dressing.

"And many resorted unto him, and said, John did no miracle: but all things that John spake of this man were true."
John 10:41

Even though John the Baptist was a rabbi (John 3:26), he did not dress like the rabbis of that time. Even his diet was very different from everyone else's (Mark 1:6).

Everything that the prophet John the Baptist did during his ministry—the way he dressed, his food, the way he preached, and the baptisms he performed—was according to God's will.

The prophet John the Baptist did not do what any other prophet had done before him or during his ministry. Instead, John did what God sent him to do and in the way that God told him to do it (John 1:33).

Genuine Christians, as children of God, will receive our identity from God, and He will bring about a change in us, discarding the old identity we had in the world to give us the new identity through His Holy Spirit.

"9. Know ye not that the unrighteous shall not inherit the kingdom of God? Be not deceived: neither fornicators, nor idolaters, nor adulterers, nor effeminate, nor abusers of themselves with mankind, 10. Nor thieves, nor covetous, nor drunkards, nor re-

vilers, nor extortioners, shall inherit the kingdom of God. 11. And such were some of you: but ye are washed, but ye are sanctified, but ye are justified in the name of the Lord Jesus, and by the Spirit of our God."
1 Corinthians 6:9-11

As children of God, our example to follow is Jesus Christ Himself.

"Till we all come in the unity of the faith, and of the knowledge of the Son of God, unto a perfect man, unto the measure of the stature of the fulness of Christ:"
Ephesians 4:13

Now let's look at another example concerning a unique identity:

"And she said, The Philistines be upon thee, Samson. And he awoke out of his sleep, and said, I will go out as at other times before, and shake myself. And he wist not that the Lord was departed from him."
Judges 16:20

Samson's strength was part of his identity. Samson was known by the Philistines for his great strength, and they feared him for that reason.

When we remember Samson or identify him in the Bible, it is not only by his name or because he had long hair, but we identify Samson by the great strength he had. However, Samson lost that strength when he disobeyed God.

God made a covenant with Samson even before he was born, and Samson had to fulfill that covenant; otherwise, he would lose his strength, as happened when his hair was cut.

"For, lo, thou shalt conceive, and bear a son; and no razor shall come on his head: for the child shall be a Nazarite unto God from the womb: and he shall begin to deliver Israel out of the hand of the Philistines."
Judges 13:5

When Samson lost his strength by disobeying God, he also lost his identity, and the same can happen to us if we separate from God.

Samson's strength was part of his identity, and that strength was given to him by God, by His Holy Spirit.

Just as Samson had his own unique identity with something that characterized and made him unique, so you and I have been created to have our own identity.

You were created to have your own identity.

Chapter 4
Three types of identity

There are three types of identity that a person could have:

1. Human identity
2. Malignant spiritual identity
3. Identity that comes from God

1. Human Identity

A person could have an identity created by themselves.

When a person copies the attitudes or behaviors of others, they are attempting to take on the identity of those other people. While they may acquire an identity, it is not genuine because it does not belong to them; this person acts as they do because they saw others behaving that way and want to be the same.

Moreover, by copying the identity, behavior, and attitudes of another person, the adopted identity will be temporary. Humans go through different stages in life, and in each stage, we change, whether in our outward appearance, way of thinking, or interests. These changes occur due to the different stages of life that humans experience.

First, we are babies, then children. Puberty follows, then youth, adulthood, and finally old age. In each of these stages, our external body changes, our perspective on life changes, and our interests change as well.

In childhood, we want to play. During adolescence and youth, our interests differ, and in adulthood, they change again.

Therefore, if a person copies something from others, the person who has copied will not be genuine for many reasons. One reason is that people are ever-changing, and even if they imitate something from another Christian, how can they be sure that person has not copied someone else? Even if that person has not copied anyone and has a genuine identity, the imitator will not be genuine. We are all unique, with different callings, purposes, and gifts.

If we want to be and do what another genuine Christian does, we will not be able to know our own identity because we will be adopting an identity that is not ours and has not been given to us by God.

Human identity is not given by God but comes from the will of man.

2. Malignant Spiritual Identity

Some people acquire an identity given by demons or evil spirits. A person possessed or influenced by these demonic entities will be known by that identity.

"26. And they arrived at the country of the Gadarenes, which is over against Galilee. 27. And when he went forth to land, there met him out of the city a certain man, which had devils long time, and ware no clothes, neither abode in any house, but in the tombs. 28. When he saw Jesus, he cried out, and fell down before him, and with a loud voice said, What have I to do with thee, Jesus, thou Son of God most high? I beseech thee, torment me not. 29. (For he had commanded the unclean spirit to come out of the man. For oftentimes it had caught him: and he was kept bound with chains and in fetters; and he brake the bands, and was driven of the devil into the wilderness.) 30. And Jesus asked him, saying, What is thy name? And he said, Legion: because many devils were entered into him."
Luke 8:26-30

We see this man who had an encounter with Jesus. This man was possessed, he was demon-possessed, and he was known throughout that region for his behaviors, qualities, and characteristics. However, the identity this man had, his way of being, was given to him by the demons that had possessed him when they entered him.

This man behaved and acted in certain ways, but not of his own will, nor was he driven by the Holy Spirit of God. He was that way because the demons inside him compelled him to be and to do what he did. In other words, that identity was given to him by evil spirits.

Evil spirits can influence a human being to adopt inappropriate attitudes and behaviors, even against their will. Nevertheless, the manner of being of this person becomes part of them and part of their personal identity.

Spirits, or demons, can influence a person, but they can also possess them, as was the case with this man from Gadara.

In our time, psychologists or psychiatrists might label such people as "crazy" when they are influenced or possessed by evil spirits. However, we see that these are people who have lost their identity due to demonic possession or influence. The identity of these people will be known by how they behave, yet the identity they have comes from evil.

We can also see that some people voluntarily seek to be influenced and possessed by evil spirits. We see this in witches, fortune-tellers, etc. These people voluntarily chose that path, but others are possessed or influenced against their will.

For this reason, every Christian must be careful about what they see, what they listen to, what they speak, what they think, and where they go, because Satan can use any of these gateways to enter a Christian's life and influence or possess them.

"26. Jesus answered, He it is, to whom I shall give a sop, when I have dipped it. And when he had dipped the sop, he gave it to Ju-

das Iscariot, the son of Simon. 27. And after the sop Satan entered into him. Then said Jesus unto him, That thou doest, do quickly."
John 13:26-27

In this scripture, we see how Satan entered Judas, but Judas had already opened spiritual doors earlier for Satan to influence him. He had opened spiritual doors because he was stealing the offerings.

"4. Then saith one of his disciples, Judas Iscariot, Simon's son, which should betray him, 5. Why was not this ointment sold for three hundred pence, and given to the poor? 6. This he said, not that he cared for the poor; but because he was a thief, and had the bag, and bare what was put therein."
John 12:4-6

This is why we must be very careful not to be influenced or possessed, as in the previously mentioned cases.

3. The Identity That Comes from God

" 1. And when Abram was ninety years old and nine, the Lord appeared to Abram, and said unto him, I am the Almighty God; walk before me, and be thou perfect. 2. And I will make my covenant between me and thee, and will multiply thee exceedingly. 3 .And Abram fell on his face: and God talked with him, saying, 4. As for me, behold, my covenant is with thee, and thou shalt be a father of many nations. 5. Neither shall thy name any more

be called Abram, but thy name shall be Abraham; for a father of many nations have I made thee."
Genesis 17:1-5

When God called Abraham, He told him to be blameless and perfect. God also changed his name from Abram to Abraham, telling him that He would make him the father of a great nation.

By making these promises and changing his name, God changed Abraham's identity.

Abraham came from a people who did not know God; he had different customs, and the people of his town knew him in a certain way, with specific qualities and characteristics. But when God called him, made promises to him, changed his name, and told him to leave the place where he lived, God made him a new man with a new identity.

If we had known Abraham before God revealed Himself to him and called him, we would have known a different Abram. Today, we know Abraham as the father of faith. We know Abraham as we do according to the Scriptures because God called him and gave him a new identity, and God does the same with each of us who are His children; He gives us a new identity.

If people once knew us as criminals, swindlers, liars, etc., now in Christ Jesus, God through His Holy Spirit changes our lives. Now, we are known by what God has done in our lives. He has changed our old lives for a new life; He has given us a new identity in Him.

> "9. Know ye not that the unrighteous shall not inherit the kingdom of God? Be not deceived: neither fornicators, nor idolaters, nor adulterers, nor effeminate, nor abusers of themselves with mankind, 10. Nor thieves, nor covetous, nor drunkards, nor revilers, nor extortioners, shall inherit the kingdom of God. 11. And such were some of you: but ye are washed, but ye are sanctified, but ye are justified in the name of the Lord Jesus, and by the Spirit of our God."
>
> 1 Corinthians 6:9-11

Let's look at another example of God's identity:

> "19. So he departed thence, and found Elisha the son of Shaphat, who was plowing with twelve yoke of oxen before him, and he with the twelfth: and Elijah passed by him, and cast his mantle upon him. 20. And he left the oxen, and ran after Elijah, and said, Let me, I pray thee, kiss my father and my mother, and then I will follow thee. And he said unto him, Go back again: for what have I done to thee? 21. And he returned back from him, and took a yoke of oxen, and slew them, and boiled their flesh with the instruments of the oxen, and gave unto the people, and they did eat. Then he arose, and went after Elijah, and ministered unto him."
>
> 1 Kings 19:19-21

Eliseo worked in the field, and the people of his place, his town, possibly knew him as a farmer who plowed the land to sow and sustain himself.

We see that Eliseo had an identity in his town, and he was known by that identity until the moment when God, through the prophet Elias, called him to be a prophet, and with that call, He also gave him a new identity.

Before being called by God, Eliseo plowed the land. Now, Eliseo would prophesy. Before, he was a farmer, and now he would be a prophet. That would be his new identity.

God wants to give us our own unique identity, just as He did with the patriarch Abraham and the prophet Eliseo, to whom He gave a new identity according to the call and purpose that God had for each of them. Likewise, God wants to give us an identity through His Spirit, and we will obtain it if we remain in His will and in communion with Him.

"4. Abide in me, and I in you. As the branch cannot bear fruit of itself, except it abide in the vine; no more can ye, except ye abide in me. 5. I am the vine, ye are the branches: He that abideth in me, and I in him, the same bringeth forth much fruit: for without me ye can do nothing."
John 15:4-5

There are three types of identity, and we will have the identity of that to which we are most attached.

If we are more attached to the world and ourselves, we will create our own identity or imitate others to resemble them and have some kind of identity.

If we are careless and look to the world, something more severe could happen—we could be influenced by demons or something worse if we seek the things of evil. That influence or demonic possession comes from evil spirits, as in the case of the demon-possessed man from Gadara (Luke 8:26-39).

But if we stay close to God and remain in His will, we will have an identity given by God Himself, through His Word and His Holy Spirit.

The question we can ask ourselves is this: What identity do we want to have?

Chapter 5
Human identity and God's Identity

All human beings are unique at birth; we all have our own characteristics, attitudes, and traits that define and distinguish us from others.

Some people, as they grow up, seek to have an identity humanly and, in that search for identity, they copy others and want to be like them to identify with them and have an identity. But if we are the ones who have wanted to be like other people, and it has not been God who has given us that identity, we will not be what we were truly born to be. Why? Because by seeking, observing, and doing what others do, we become imitators and not genuine.

We will adopt a little from each person and grow up with a fake identity, formed by pieces or parts of the identities of other people. It is even likely that these people have done the same thing previously, imitating others.

A person who has copied someone else to have their own identity will not be genuine. Before God, this person will be someone without a true identity.

That is why, when God comes into our lives, we enter a process with God for Him to shape us and give us our identity.

God created us to have our own identity. As children of God, He shapes us, repairs our souls, changes our minds, and our inner selves as only He knows how, making us into what He wants us to be.

We will start like a baby, seeing as God wants us to see and being as God wants us to be. We will begin to hear as God wants us to hear, speak what He wants us to speak, think as He wants us to think, go where He wants us to go, and do things the way He wants us to do them.

We will start learning little by little and will be shaped in our spirit with the help of the Holy Spirit to have the identity that God wants to give each of us individually.

In God, and with God, we will learn to be as God wants us to be, and we will become what He wants us to be; for this purpose, God will use His Word and the power of His Spirit.

"Thy word is a lamp unto my feet, and a light unto my path."
Psalms 119:105

"22. That ye put off concerning the former conversation the old man, which is corrupt according to the deceitful lusts; 23. And be renewed in the spirit of your mind; 24. And that ye put on the new man, which after God is created in righteousness and true holiness."
Ephesians 4:22-24

God will also use His Spirit to reveal things to us:

"But the anointing which ye have received of him abideth in you, and ye need not that any man teach you: but as the same anointing teacheth you of all things, and is truth, and is no lie, and even as it hath taught you, ye shall abide in him."
1 John 2:27

God will also use situations and circumstances in our lives as Christians to shape us and give us a new and unique identity.

When we were in the world without God, the examples and prototypes of identity we had were the most influential people we knew or saw. These could have been well-known people in the secular world, but they could also have been friends, and we used all these references to form and have our own identity.

But when we were known by God, and He called us to salvation, our example and reference for identity became Jesus, the Messiah.

"Be ye followers of me, even as I also am of Christ."
1 Corinthians 11:1

Now our example is Christ, and Christ will help us with the power of His Holy Spirit to become and have our identity in Him, as well as our identity and position in His church, the body of Christ.

> *"For we are his workmanship, created in Christ Jesus unto good works, which God hath before ordained that we should walk in them."*
> Ephesians 2:10

Only God can give us a genuine and true identity and shape it through His Holy Spirit and His Word.

In the world, many of us believed we were someone, that we had an identity, but when we were known by God, we realized we were blind and lost.

The identity of the world is not genuine. The identity many of us had in the world was a copy of someone else, of another person or other people. Likewise, we may have been the copy for someone else.

A person can only have a genuine identity when it is given by God; otherwise, they are merely imitating others.

When God created man, He created him with a unique and individual identity.

Let's look at the case of Adam:

> *"And out of the ground the Lord God formed every beast of the field, and every fowl of the air; and brought them unto Adam to see what he would call them: and whatsoever Adam called every living creature, that was the name thereof."*
> Genesis 2:19

The Word of God says that God brought animals and birds of the sky to Adam to name them.

This is an example of how God made Adam and formed him with a specific purpose.

If we stay close to God and remain near Him, we will know our identity and be able to obtain it. But if we are far from God, we will not know our identity and will not be able to obtain it.

Every genuine Christian, if they distance themselves from God and His will, will lose the identity they had when they were close to God. They will only regain that identity when they return to God with all their heart.

Man lost his identity when he separated from God because of the sin he committed.

Let's look at two examples:

Example #1

"8. And Cain talked with Abel his brother: and it came to pass, when they were in the field, that Cain rose up against Abel his brother, and slew him. 9. And the Lord said unto Cain, Where is Abel thy brother? And he said, I know not: Am I my brother's keeper? 10. And he said, What hast thou done? the voice of thy brother's blood crieth unto me from the ground. 11. And now art thou cursed from the earth, which hath opened her mouth to receive thy brother's blood from thy hand; 12. When thou tillest the ground,

*it shall not henceforth yield unto thee her strength; a fugitive and a vagabond shalt thou be in the earth. 13. And Cain said unto the Lord, My punishment is greater than I can bear. 14. Behold, thou hast driven me out this day from the face of the earth; and from thy face shall I be hid; and I shall be a fugitive and a vagabond in the earth; and it shall come to pass, that every one that findeth me shall slay me. 15. And the Lord said unto him, Therefore whosoever slayeth Cain, vengeance shall be taken on him sevenfold. And the Lord set a mark upon Cain, lest any finding him should kill him."
Genesis 4:8-15*

Cain was the first son of Adam and Eve, and we can also see that Cain had a relationship with God in some respects. We see that Cain, like his younger brother Abel, offered a sacrifice to God. Additionally, we observe that God speaks to Cain and explains why He did not accept his offering. This relationship between God and Cain was broken when Cain sinned against God by killing his brother Abel.

After that event, Cain was banished by God, and he left the place where he was. Cain understood that God's presence would no longer be with him. He had to find a new place and start a new life.

The sin Cain committed resulted in God's punishment, and Cain was given a new identity—one without God.

Example #2

"16. Unto the woman he said, I will greatly multiply thy sorrow and thy conception; in sorrow thou shalt bring forth children;

and thy desire shall be to thy husband, and he shall rule over thee. 17. And unto Adam he said, Because thou hast hearkened unto the voice of thy wife, and hast eaten of the tree, of which I commanded thee, saying, Thou shalt not eat of it: cursed is the ground for thy sake; in sorrow shalt thou eat of it all the days of thy life; 18. Thorns also and thistles shall it bring forth to thee; and thou shalt eat the herb of the field; 19. In the sweat of thy face shalt thou eat bread, till thou return unto the ground; for out of it wast thou taken: for dust thou art, and unto dust shalt thou return."
Genesis 3:16-19

The punishment God gave to Adam and Eve for their disobedience resulted in a different kind of life, an inferior life compared to what they had before. It would be a life filled with suffering and pain. They could now only hope for God's mercy. From that moment on, anyone who approached God with all their heart could be restored and given a new life, a new identity with the help of God and the power of His Holy Spirit.

This has not changed. In the current time we live in, God has sent His only Son, Jesus, the Messiah, the Savior of the world. To anyone who believes in Him and lives for Him, He will give a new life, a new identity—the identity that our first parents, Adam and Eve, lost in Eden due to their disobedience.

"Wherefore, as by one man sin entered into the world, and death by sin; and so death passed upon all men, for that all have sinned"
Romans 5:12

"18. Therefore as by the offence of one judgment came upon all men to condemnation; even so by the righteousness of one the free gift came upon all men unto justification of life. 19. For as by one man's disobedience many were made sinners, so by the obedience of one shall many be made righteous."
Romans 5:18-19

We can understand, then, that through Jesus Christ we can all have a new life, a new identity—the identity lost by our first parents, Adam and Eve. This identity can be restored to us through Jesus Christ by His Holy Spirit.

When we do not have an identity given through Jesus, by His Word and His Spirit, we wander aimlessly, without identity. We will be searching here and there to obtain some form of identity.

We conclude, therefore, that human identity is temporary, fictitious, superficial, false, and not genuine. It is also a fallen, earthly identity, from below.

"46. Howbeit that was not first which is spiritual, but that which is natural; and afterward that which is spiritual. 47. The first man is of the earth, earthy; the second man is the Lord from heaven. 48. As is the earthy, such are they also that are earthy: and as is the heavenly, such are they also that are heavenly. 49. And as we have borne the image of the earthy, we shall also bear the image of the heavenly."
1 Corinthians 15:46-49

The identity that God wants to give us is a heavenly, divine, and eternal identity, in the image of Christ.

When we are on God's path and remain on that path, we are in His hands, being formed by Him, by His Holy Spirit, by His Word. We are being transformed day by day to become what God wants us to be.

"For which cause we faint not; but though our outward man perish, yet the inward man is renewed day by day."
2 Corinthians 4:16

"5. Then the word of the Lord came to me, saying, 6. O house of Israel, cannot I do with you as this potter? saith the Lord. Behold, as the clay is in the potter's hand, so are ye in mine hand, O house of Israel."
Jeremiah 18:5-6

If you are on God's path and stay on that path, you will also be in God's process, and just as He gave an identity to the patriarchs and prophets, He will give you a unique and genuine identity.

Only God can give us a true and genuine identity.

Chapter 6
Internal and external identity

"And the very God of peace sanctify you wholly; and I pray God your whole spirit and soul and body be preserved blameless unto the coming of our Lord Jesus Christ."
1 Thessalonians 5:23

Many people outwardly appear to be a certain way, but in their hearts, they are not what they seem on the outside. This can be defined as people having an identity, a particularity, a way of being in their interior, in their heart, but externally they are different types of people.

Other people may have an opinion of this person based on the appearance they show outwardly, but the person who shows themselves this way externally may be very different on the inside.

In the world, it is common and normal to see these cases and situations—people who appear a certain way, in a certain form, but are not truly that way on the inside.

We can also see these cases within the realm of Christianity.

Many of us, upon converting to Christianity and starting God's process, present an image of being Christians, but in our hearts or minds, we may not necessarily be that way. In our hearts and minds, we are still struggling to be genuine Christians. Or it can happen with another group of Christians, whose hearts and minds are still in the world.

This can happen for three reasons:

1. Because we are in God's process and still need to be changed by the Holy Spirit of God, and we must continue so that God completes His work.

"Being confident of this very thing, that he which hath begun a good work in you will perform it until the day of Jesus Christ:"
Philippians 1:6

2. Because we have not genuinely surrendered to God, and for that reason, God has not changed our lives.

"37. Now when they heard this, they were pricked in their heart, and said unto Peter and to the rest of the apostles, Men and brethren, what shall we do? 38. Then Peter said unto them, Repent, and be baptized every one of you in the name of Jesus Christ for the remission of sins, and ye shall receive the gift of the Holy Ghost."
Acts 2:37-38

God will change and transform us when our surrender is genuine and sincere. Then, the Spirit of God will descend, enter our hearts, and begin the process of change in our lives.

3. We may have been changed by the Spirit of God, but we have distanced ourselves from Him. We might still attend church and call ourselves Christians, but our hearts are far from God.

"Then said he unto me, Son of man, hast thou seen what the ancients of the house of Israel do in the dark, every man in the chambers of his imagery? for they say, the Lord seeth us not; the Lord hath forsaken the earth."
Ezekiel 8:12

The priests of Israel, although called and chosen by God, had an outward identity before the congregation of the children of Israel. However, in secret, they were different people, and no one knew this except God.

If you or I had lived during that time, we too could have been deceived just like the people of that time, unless we had received a revelation of that situation like the prophet Ezekiel did (Ezekiel 8:12). We would have thought their identity was that of impeccable priests, but in reality, it was an external image they showed to the people. In their homes, in their chambers, they were different people.

When a Christian is not close to God and in communion with Him, they can lose what they have gained as a child of God. They might even appear to have a spiritual relationship with God when they no longer do. They can present themselves to people as if they are in communion with God, but it is not so in their spirit.

A genuine identity begins in our heart, and that identity will become visible in our exterior.

It is like a person who speaks many words but has no faith in what they speak. This person talks, proclaims, and does many things, but they do it without genuine faith.

"8. But what saith it? The word is nigh thee, even in thy mouth, and in thy heart: that is, the word of faith, which we preach; 9. That if thou shalt confess with thy mouth the Lord Jesus, and shalt believe in thine heart that God hath raised him from the dead, thou shalt be saved. 10. For with the heart man believeth unto righteousness; and with the mouth confession is made unto salvation."
Romans 10:8-10

Faith starts in our hearts, but many of us speak words without faith.

Our heart, our interior, and our exterior must be one; they must be united. This is when we will be genuine children of God, genuine Christians, because we will be known in a certain way outwardly and be that way in our hearts, in our homes, where no one can see us.

The Spirit of God will work with each of us to be genuine both internally and externally.

"And the very God of peace sanctify you wholly; and I pray God your whole spirit and soul and body be preserved blameless unto the coming of our Lord Jesus Christ."
1 Thessalonians 5:23

We must be genuine where everyone sees us and likewise where no one sees us (except God). Then we will be true children of God.

"9. Know ye not that the unrighteous shall not inherit the kingdom of God? Be not deceived: neither fornicators, nor idolaters, nor adulterers, nor effeminate, nor abusers of themselves with mankind, 10. Nor thieves, nor covetous, nor drunkards, nor revilers, nor extortioners, shall inherit the kingdom of God. 11. And such were some of you: but ye are washed, but ye are sanctified, but ye are justified in the name of the Lord Jesus, and by the Spirit of our God."
1 Corinthians 6:9-11

The apostle Paul reminds the brothers of the church in Corinth that before knowing the Lord, they had different lives, lives full of sin. Some were drunkards and were known that way; others were known for being criminals; and so on with each person. These were some of the identities that some of them had, but upon converting to God, He changed and transformed them. The apostle Paul reminds them of this because possibly some were falling into insincerity and still calling themselves Christians, having a double standard.

In the book of 1 Corinthians 5, the apostle Paul urges them to be genuine in their Christian lives, not to have a double standard, a double identity, and not to appear to be true Christians without actually being so.

As Christians, we must strive to be obedient to the Word of God. This will help us be genuine in our Christianity, both internally and externally. But we must strive to be obedient to the Spirit of God, as it is the Holy Spirit who will convict us of sin and change us both internally and externally.

"And when he is come, he will reprove the world of sin, and of righteousness, and of judgment:"
John 16:8

If the Holy Spirit does not change us from within, we cannot be genuine but will be hypocrites like the Pharisees, who opposed the ministry of Jesus, the Messiah. They were outwardly clean but not in their hearts.

"27. Woe unto you, scribes and Pharisees, hypocrites! for ye are like unto whited sepulchres, which indeed appear beautiful outward, but are within full of dead men's bones, and of all uncleanness. 28. Even so ye also outwardly appear righteous unto men, but within ye are full of hypocrisy and iniquity."
Matthew 23:27-28

The Jews in the time of Jesus, who belonged to a religion or sect, such as the Pharisees, the Sadducees, etc., had a double standard. They outwardly appeared to be what they were not internally.

This can also happen to each of us if we are not sincere with God and have not genuinely surrendered our lives to Him. We can appear to be true followers of Christ outwardly, giving that impression, but in reality, we might be living outside God's will, living in sin, and not being transformed or renewed in our hearts.

A genuine Christian must have only one identity and be genuine in the identity they have as a child of God. They must be the same inside and out, not having a double standard.

Our identity is based on the Word of God and is given by the Holy Spirit of God.

If a Christian has a calling from God to be a preacher, prophet, or to have any other ministry, and this person, despite having the calling, is not true in their interior, their ministry will be weak and have a double standard. Outwardly, they will be known for their ministry, but in their spirit, they will not truly believe it.

For a person to be strong in their ministry and the calling they have from God, they must believe in their calling, be sincere in their heart, and not pretend outwardly before others.

A true disciple of Christ, a true minister of God, will be respected and genuine before others when they are first genuine in their heart and consequently in their outward, public life. People, seeing the testimony of this person's life, will believe in their calling and in their Christianity.

The Holy Spirit will work in our hearts to change and shape us according to His will.

"He that overcometh, the same shall be clothed in white raiment; and I will not blot out his name out of the book of life, but I will confess his name before my Father, and before his angels." Revelation 3:5

In the Kingdom of Heaven, God will give each of us new clothes, but He will also give us a new name.

When God gives us a new identity, He does so both inside and out.

Chapter 7
Our personality is not our identity

We all have our own personality. Some people have a more extroverted, open personality, while others may have a more introverted and shy personality.

For some, having a more extroverted personality will help in certain areas of their lives, while for others, that personality may not be as beneficial.

However, our personality, whatever it may be, is not our identity. It can be a part of it, but it is not everything.

In the Scriptures, we can see men who did not have a great personality but did have an identity, and that identity was given to them by God.

"And Moses said unto the Lord, O my Lord, I am not eloquent, neither heretofore, nor since thou hast spoken unto thy servant: but I am slow of speech, and of a slow tongue."
Exodus 4:10

In the previously cited text, we read that Moses had difficulty speaking and communicating with others. However, if we look at Moses' ministry as a prophet of God, we can see that he was known and is still known as one of the greatest prophets in biblical history. Despite Moses not having an extroverted personality or eloquence in communicating with people, God gave him an identity, and along with that identity, He gave him signs, wonders, and miracles that were part of his ministry. Because of all this, we know Moses as a great prophet of God.

"26. For ye see your calling, brethren, how that not many wise men after the flesh, not many mighty, not many noble, are called: 27. But God hath chosen the foolish things of the world to confound the wise; and God hath chosen the weak things of the world to confound the things which are mighty; 28. And base things of the world, and things which are despised, hath God chosen, yea, and things which are not, to bring to nought things that are: 29. That no flesh should glory in his presence."
1 Corinthians 1:26-29

In these cited texts, the apostle Paul tells us the type of people God has chosen—those who were despised and had no value to the world.

People like Moses, who were not eloquent, or those who were shy, introverted, and even had many complexes, as I was before knowing God, are the ones God has called and given an identity to, just as He gave to Moses, the patriarchs, and the prophets of the Old Testament.

Personality is rooted in our soul, and only God can transform us. Even if our personality is like Moses' or even more lacking, if God gives us an identity, we will be what God wants us to be.

Often, God may allow our poor personality so that He Himself is glorified through us in those weaknesses.

"7. And lest I should be exalted above measure through the abundance of the revelations, there was given to me a thorn in the flesh, the messenger of Satan to buffet me, lest I should be exalted above measure. 8. For this thing I besought the Lord thrice, that it might depart from me. 9. And he said unto me, My grace is sufficient for thee: for my strength is made perfect in weakness. Most gladly therefore will I rather glory in my infirmities, that the power of Christ may rest upon me. 10. Therefore I take pleasure in infirmities, in reproaches, in necessities, in persecutions, in distresses for Christ's sake: for when I am weak, then am I strong"
2 Corinthians 12:7-10

God can glorify Himself in our weaknesses, just as He did with Paul or with Moses.

We may have a good personality, be eloquent, etc., but if God has not given us an identity in Him, we will only be attractive or known for having traits that draw other people. On the other hand, we can be very shy and not have a clear identity.

"And I, brethren, when I came to you, came not with excellency of speech or of wisdom, declaring unto you the testimony of God."
1 Corinthians 2:1

"And my speech and my preaching was not with enticing words of man's wisdom, but in demonstration of the Spirit and of power:"
1 Corinthians 2:4

Our personality is human, but our identity comes from God.

Our personality needs to be shaped and refined by God through His Word and His Holy Spirit.

"And be not conformed to this world: but be ye transformed by the renewing of your mind, that ye may prove what is that good, and acceptable, and perfect, will of God."
Romans 12:2

"22. That ye put off concerning the former conversation the old man, which is corrupt according to the deceitful lusts; 23. And be renewed in the spirit of your mind; 24. And that ye put on the new man, which after God is created in righteousness and true holiness."
Ephesians 4:22-24

Our identity needs to be changed into a new identity.

Many people have human talents—they may play a musical instrument; others speak well and express themselves well, and that is part of each person. We all can have human qualities or talents, but as Christians, we must know and understand that apart from the human talents each person may have, God also wants to give us an identity.

If God does not give us an identity as His children, everything we do as Christians will be based on our own human abilities, talents, or qualities, but it will not be spiritual. If God has not given me the ministry of preaching or playing instruments and singing praises, and I still do it, those preachings or praises will not be spiritual but human.

We may have human talents or qualities, but all that is human. This is why there are secular music singers, teachers who teach someone how to sing, how to speak, how to express themselves before an audience, etc., but those are only human things.

God wants to give us something more.

When God gives us a new identity, and if He has called us to praise Him, He will anoint us to praise Him. If we do not know how to express ourselves well or speak well, but God has called us to preach, He will anoint us with His Holy Spirit and give us the right words to speak, and He will teach us the right way to speak them. It will not be us with our personality or human talents, but God Himself doing it through His Holy Spirit.

Our personality is human and must be refined.

Our identity comes from God and is given by God.

Our identity is heavenly.

It is not so important if we have one personality or another. When we genuinely surrender to God, God, through His Holy Spirit, will work in us to give us a new identity that was prepared and designed for each one of us. It will not be our human talents that we already have, nor will it be our introverted or extroverted personality, but it will be given by the Holy Spirit of God—it will be something much greater.

The personality we all have is not our identity.

The identity given by God, through His Holy Spirit, is not our own.

We can have a very good personality, but if God does not give us an identity, everything we do will be of ourselves, and we will be known not for what God has done or is doing through us, but for our human talents and abilities.

However, we may not have an outstanding personality, but if God gives us an identity, we will be known for what God does through us, His power acting through us.

In conclusion, we should not think that our personality can take the place or position of the new identity that God wants to give us. What God wants to give us, or what He has already given us, is spiritual and comes from God, not from us. Our personality is human, natural, and is part of our identity, but it is not our identity.

We should also know that if we have a very introverted personality, or on the contrary, a very extroverted one, when God gives us an identity, we will be complete, and our personality will adapt to our identity.

In the process of being formed by God's Word and His Spirit, our personality will be refined to become part of our new identity.

Remember:

Personality is human and needs to be refined and perfected.

Identity is from God and comes from above, from heaven.

A prophet is known for being a prophet, and that is his identity. He can be very extroverted or very conservative.

A pastor or an evangelist each has a personality, but they will be known by people for their calling or ministry.

A person may have a personality and think that their personality is their identity, but that is not the case. Our personality is not our identity, but it is part of our identity.

Our personality needs to be shaped to become part of our identity.

Chapter 8
In a new identity comes something new from God

Identity is defined as the qualities, traits, aptitudes, or characteristics of a person that distinguish them from another person.

When we genuinely and sincerely receive Jesus into our hearts, we also receive the Holy Spirit.

"37. Now when they heard this, they were pricked in their heart, and said unto Peter and to the rest of the apostles, Men and brethren, what shall we do? 38. Then Peter said unto them, Repent, and be baptized every one of you in the name of Jesus Christ for the remission of sins, and ye shall receive the gift of the Holy Ghost."
Acts 2:37-38

With the coming of the Spirit of God also come the gifts or unique ministries that God has already prepared for us individually.

These gifts or ministries that God, through His Holy Spirit, will give each of us will be like a sign that identifies us, and that will be part of our identity.

In the book of 1 Corinthians 12, the apostle Paul speaks to us about spiritual gifts and also about the ministries that the Holy Spirit gives to each person. He also clarifies that they will be given according to how the Holy Spirit wills.

Each of us will have a gift, ministry, or manifestation of the Spirit for the benefit of God's people.

We can see in the Old Testament that God gave His servants something that identified them, and they were recognized for what they had received from God.

For example, God called Abram and gave him a new name.

"1. And when Abram was ninety years old and nine, the Lord appeared to Abram, and said unto him, I am the Almighty God; walk before me, and be thou perfect. 2. And I will make my covenant between me and thee, and will multiply thee exceedingly. 3. And Abram fell on his face: and God talked with him, saying, 4. As for me, behold, my covenant is with thee, and thou shalt be a father of many nations. 5. Neither shall thy name any more be called Abram, but thy name shall be Abraham; for a father of many nations have I made thee."
Genesis 17:1-5

God gave Abram a new name; He said his new name would be Abraham and told him that He had given him this new name because now he would be the father of many nations. By promising Abram something and changing his name to Abraham, God also gave him a new identity.

Let's look at another example:

"24. And Jacob was left alone; and there wrestled a man with him until the breaking of the day. 25. And when he saw that he prevailed not against him, he touched the hollow of his thigh; and the hollow of Jacob's thigh was out of joint, as he wrestled with him. 26. And he said, Let me go, for the day breaketh. And he said, I will not let thee go, except thou bless me. 27. And he said unto him, What is thy name? And he said, Jacob. 28. And he said, Thy name shall be called no more Jacob, but Israel: for as a prince hast thou power with God and with men, and hast prevailed." Genesis 32:24-28

God gave Jacob a new name to form a nation through him, which would be called Israel, and that became Jacob's new name, Israel.

Now, Jacob would no longer be the same as before; he was a new person, with a new name, and that new name was part of his new identity.

We can also see the case of Sarai, Abraham's wife, and how God changed her name as a sign of her new identity.

"15. And God said unto Abraham, As for Sarai thy wife, thou shalt not call her name Sarai, but Sarah shall her name be. 16. And I will bless her, and give thee a son also of her: yea, I will

bless her, and she shall be a mother of nations; kings of people shall be of her."
Genesis 17:15-16

When God gives us a new identity, He will also do something new in us, which will be part of our new identity.

Now let's look at the case of Samson. We usually identify Samson because he was someone who had great strength; that was what identified him.

"5. Then went Samson down, and his father and his mother, to Timnath, and came to the vineyards of Timnath: and, behold, a young lion roared against him. 6. And the Spirit of the Lord came mightily upon him, and he rent him as he would have rent a kid, and he had nothing in his hand: but he told not his father or his mother what he had done."
Judges 14:5-6

This was the sign that identified Samson as someone unique, and this sign was from God, given by God Himself to Samson.

We can also observe the case of King Solomon:

"10. And the speech pleased the Lord, that Solomon had asked this thing. 11. And God said unto him, Because thou hast asked this thing, and hast not asked for thyself long life; neither hast asked riches for thyself, nor hast asked the life of thine enemies; but hast asked for thyself understanding to discern judgment; 12. Behold, I have done according to thy words: lo, I have given thee

a wise and an understanding heart; so that there was none like thee before thee, neither after thee shall any arise like unto thee. 13. And I have also given thee that which thou hast not asked, both riches, and honour: so that there shall not be any among the kings like unto thee all thy days."
1 Kings 3:10-13

Among the many things God gave Solomon, He gave him wisdom.

The wisdom that Solomon had was part of his identity as a person. We can see in the Bible all that Solomon wrote through the wisdom that God had given him. If we want to mention a man who had great wisdom and is written about in the Holy Scriptures, that man would be Solomon.

We could continue listing the men and women of God and what God gave them as a sign, which was part of their identities.

We can also see how Jesus changed Simon's name to Peter as a sign of what God would do with him.

"41. He first findeth his own brother Simon, and saith unto him, We have found the Messias, which is, being interpreted, the Christ. 42. And he brought him to Jesus. And when Jesus beheld him, he said, Thou art Simon the son of Jona: thou shalt be called Cephas, which is by interpretation, A stone."
John 1:41-42

Let's see what will change when we are transformed and go to be with the Eternal Father:

"He that hath an ear, let him hear what the Spirit saith unto the churches; To him that overcometh will I give to eat of the hidden manna, and will give him a white stone, and in the stone a new name written, which no man knoweth saving he that receiveth it."
Revelation 2:17

God will give each of us a new name, which will be part of our new celestial identity, where we will live with God for eternity.

We can see in the Bible, in the writings of the prophets and other authors, that each one was different and characterized by something unique that God gave them, whether prophets, scribes, or apostles.

The Holy Spirit will give each of us a gift, a ministry, or may even change our name to a new one as part of our new identity. If we are in communion with the Father, we will be able to know and recognize the new things that God has given us, which will be part of our new identity. However, if we are not in communion with the Father through the Spirit of God, we will not be able to discern or recognize it.

"10. And his disciples asked him, saying, Why then say the scribes that Elias must first come? 11. And Jesus answered and said unto them, Elias truly shall first come, and restore all things. 12. But I say unto you, That Elias is come already, and they knew

him not, but have done unto him whatsoever they listed. Likewise shall also the Son of man suffer of them. 13. Then the disciples understood that he spake unto them of John the Baptist."
Matthew 17:10-13

John the Baptist was destined by God to come and prepare the way for Jesus, the Messiah, but the prophecy says he would come with the spirit of Elijah (Luke 1:17).

Why did Jesus say that men did not recognize him? Because they did not understand that scripture, it was not revealed to them because they did not have communion with God, with His Spirit, and with His Word.

You may receive and have something new that God has given or is giving you, but in addition to receiving it, you must be in communion with God and His Word to know and understand what is new that God has given you as part of your new identity.

When God called me to preach, He did not let me know that He had given me something new, but as time passed and I had communion with God, the Lord made me know that I have a name with which I would be identified in my ministry, and that name is John. He gave me that name as a spiritual sign, like John the Baptist.

God will give us something new for our new identity as His children, but since it is from God, who is Spirit, He will reveal it to us through His Holy Spirit. Whether it is a new name like Jacob or Abraham, wisdom like He gave to Solomon, a ministry, or a gift (1 Corinthians 12), it will come only by the will of God, and He will make it known to us through His Spirit.

"9. But as it is written, Eye hath not seen, nor ear heard, neither have entered into the heart of man, the things which God hath prepared for them that love him. 10. But God hath revealed them unto us by his Spirit: for the Spirit searcheth all things, yea, the deep things of God. 11. For what man knoweth the things of a man, save the spirit of man which is in him? even so the things of God knoweth no man, but the Spirit of God. 12. Now we have received, not the spirit of the world, but the spirit which is of God; that we might know the things that are freely given to us of God."
1 Corinthians 2:9-12

Everyone who genuinely converts to God will receive something from God, and what they have received will identify them.

Chapter 9
Losing to Gain

Losing Our Old Identity to Gain a New Identity

In God's process, as we begin to live a new life in Christ as children of God, we will have to lose our previous identity to obtain our new identity. We should not cling to the identity we had in the world before becoming Christians. We must be flexible and accept the new identity, the new way of life that God wants to give us.

This process will take time; it could be months or it could be years. Some will complete this process, while others will not.

In the Scriptures, we can see some examples of God's people in their transition to receive a new life, and with that new life, also a new identity.

Let's examine the case of the people of Israel when they were brought out of Egypt.

The people of Israel had been waiting for God's deliverance for many years until God raised a deliverer, Moses.

Moses was called and chosen by God to bring the people of Israel out and lead them to the land that God had promised them. Before being freed, the people of Israel had been slaves in the nation of Egypt. The Israelites served the Egyptians; they were herdsmen or cultivated the land, but in addition to that, the Egyptians made them their slaves. That was the life they had in Egypt before being liberated by God.

"13. And the Egyptians made the children of Israel to serve with rigour: 14. And they made their lives bitter with hard bondage, in morter, and in brick, and in all manner of service in the field: all their service, wherein they made them serve, was with rigour."
Exodus 1:13-14

God sent Moses to bring His people out of Egypt, to take them from the hard life they had to a life full of abundance and with God's protection. In addition, in that new life, God would give them a new identity; they would no longer be known as slaves but as a people chosen and blessed by God.

Although God fulfilled His promise to the descendants of Abraham, Isaac, and Jacob, not all entered the new land that God had promised them. Most of those who left Egypt remained in the transition of God's process. While they stopped being slaves of Egypt, they could not enter or obtain God's promise, and with that promise, they also could not obtain a new life.

"26. And the Lord spake unto Moses and unto Aaron, saying, 27. How long shall I bear with this evil congregation, which mur-

mur against me? I have heard the murmurings of the children of Israel, which they murmur against me. 28. Say unto them, As truly as I live, saith the Lord, as ye have spoken in mine ears, so will I do to you: 29. Your carcases shall fall in this wilderness; and all that were numbered of you, according to your whole number, from twenty years old and upward which have murmured against me. 30. Doubtless ye shall not come into the land, concerning which I sware to make you dwell therein, save Caleb the son of Jephunneh, and Joshua the son of Nun. 31. But your little ones, which ye said should be a prey, them will I bring in, and they shall know the land which ye have despised. 32. But as for you, your carcases, they shall fall in this wilderness."
Numbers 14:26-32

Many Christians, children of God, do not reach their new identity in God; instead, they get stuck along the way, stalled in the transition process to the new life that God wants to give them, and they fail to obtain it.

Losing to gain: losing the old identity we had in the world to obtain a new identity as children of God.

God's people could not obtain God's promise due to their disobedience and lack of total dependence on God. They died along the way. Some died with a slave mentality, and others without knowing their purpose in God's process.

To obtain our new identity given by God through His Word and by His Spirit, we must be in continuous dependence on God, in constant pursuit and dedication to His knowledge and His Spirit.

In the book of Genesis, chapter 37, we see how Joseph is sold by his brothers. Joseph had a life with his father and his brothers, and although Joseph was a righteous young man, he still had to go through God's process to then be positioned into the new life that God had for him.

When Joseph was sold by his brothers, he was 17 years old. At that moment, the change began, God's process to give him a new life, a new identity according to God's purpose for him.

Joseph was a slave in the nation of Egypt, and in addition to that, he was imprisoned, accused of a crime he had not committed (Genesis 39). Although Joseph's life was hard, God was using all those situations to lead him to his new life, and thus give him a new identity.

Joseph went through God's process correctly and was positioned, reaching the promise that God had given him many years earlier in dreams.

The process Joseph went through lasted thirteen years. Many times Joseph must have felt alone, not being with his family, and being a slave in a foreign country with a different language; at other times, he must have felt without identity, questioning himself: "Why am I doing this? I am not a slave, but I live like a slave."

But Joseph was going through the transition to the new life that God had for him, and God was preparing him to have a new identity.

After thirteen years, Joseph is positioned and receives what God had reserved for him (Genesis 41).

When we are in God's process, in the path of losing to gain, of losing our old identity to obtain a new identity, we will often feel like we lack a defined identity.

Joseph had been sold as a slave, but he had never been a slave; all of that was new to him. However, in that process of transition, of change, God was processing him so that Joseph would see life from a different perspective, so that Joseph would think, speak, act, and do things according to the model and the new life that God was going to give him.

Joseph's father, Jacob, also had to go through a process with God, and through that process, Jacob received God's blessing, and with that blessing, Jacob obtained his new identity.

"24. And Jacob was left alone; and there wrestled a man with him until the breaking of the day. 25. And when he saw that he prevailed not against him, he touched the hollow of his thigh; and the hollow of Jacob's thigh was out of joint, as he wrestled with him. 26. And he said, Let me go, for the day breaketh. And he said, I will not let thee go, except thou bless me. 27. And he said unto him, What is thy name? And he said, Jacob. 28. And he said, Thy name shall be called no more Jacob, but Israel: for as a prince hast thou power with God and with men, and hast prevailed."
Genesis 32:24-28

In the process of losing to gain, of leaving our old life and our old identity to gain and obtain a new life and a new identity, we may feel that we do not have a defined or clear identity.

This happens because we are being changed, we are going through a transition, and in that process, we are leaving behind the identity we had in the world, our past life. However, in this stage of transition, we also do not have a new identity yet, as we are still in the process of change. Although this is already done in the spiritual world, we still need to reach it and obtain it in the natural world.

It's like an adolescent. When they are in that stage of change, entering the stage of becoming a young adult, they are leaving one stage to enter and establish themselves in a new stage in their life.

This is why most adolescents feel that very few people understand them, and in addition to that, they do not yet have established maturity, as they are still in a stage of change.

Returning to the example of Jacob, his transition process from being Jacob to becoming Israel, the nation that God would make through him, lasted 20 years (Genesis 31:36-42). In this process of ceasing to be Jacob and becoming Israel, God was changing him and giving him what he would need to reach God's promise.

The Lord Jesus said this:

"26. If any man come to me, and hate not his father, and mother, and wife, and children, and brethren, and sisters, yea, and his own life also, he cannot be my disciple. 27. And whosoever doth not bear his cross, and come after me, cannot be my disciple."
Luke 14:26-27

It is necessary to lose, to let go of our past life and our old identity, to obtain a new life, a new identity given by God.

Many times, as we leave our old life and with it our old identity, we will feel as if we are neither here nor there. This is because we are in the midst of the process of change.

Although we know in our hearts that we are children of God and that God is on our side, as we leave our old life and identity, we will feel incomplete. This is natural; we are changing, yearning to fully become what God wants us to be. If we persevere, if we persist and cling to God, just as Joshua and Caleb did, just as Jacob did, if we persevere in God's will and seek Him, we will achieve it. We will obtain God's promises for our lives, and God will also give us a new identity.

"4. Abide in me, and I in you. As the branch cannot bear fruit of itself, except it abide in the vine; no more can ye, except ye abide in me. 5. I am the vine, ye are the branches: He that abideth in me, and I in him, the same bringeth forth much fruit: for without me ye can do nothing."
John 15:4-5

All the children of God will go through this process, this transition, of losing to gain.

Consider the prophet Daniel, who had to be taken captive and leave his nation. However, we also see how God gives him a new position, and with that new position, Daniel also gains a new identity as a counselor to the king (Daniel 1).

If we persevere in seeking God and remain in His will, we will become what God wants us to be and obtain what God wants us to obtain. But if we do not persevere, if we do not stay in God's will and distance ourselves from God, we could end our days like the people of Israel. They died in the wilderness and did not receive the promise.

"28. Say unto them, As truly as I live, saith the Lord, as ye have spoken in mine ears, so will I do to you: 29. Your carcases shall fall in this wilderness; and all that were numbered of you, according to your whole number, from twenty years old and upward which have murmured against me. 30. Doubtless ye shall not come into the land, concerning which I sware to make you dwell therein, save Caleb the son of Jephunneh, and Joshua the son of Nun."
Numbers 14:28-30

Let's be like Joshua and Caleb, believe in God, hold on to Him, and we will obtain all His promises, the life, and the identity He has for us.

Lose the old identity to gain a new identity given by God.

Chapter 10
The Adversary doesn't want you to have identity

Jesus descended from heaven to give us a new life, a new identity, but Satan wants to take it away from us. He does not want us to achieve the identity that God wants to give us through His Son Jesus, by His Holy Spirit.

"The thief cometh not, but for to steal, and to kill, and to destroy: I am come that they might have life, and that they might have it more abundantly."
John 10:10

If we do not achieve our identity as children of God, we will feel incomplete.

This is why Satan and his demons will try to prevent us from having our identity as children of God, thereby frustrating us and making us feel incomplete. And if he cannot prevent it, he will try to make us lose the identity we already have as children of God, just as he did with Adam and Eve (Genesis 3).

Adam and Eve had an identity as children of God. Satan could not prevent them from having that identity since they were created by God Himself, who made them perfect and complete. They did not need to be processed from one life to another to be what God wanted them to be. They never knew human evil until the day of their transgression.

Satan could not prevent that, but he tried to make them lose the identity they already had, and he succeeded by making them fall into disobedience to God.

If Satan cannot prevent us from having our identity as children of God, and we become what God wants us to be, he will try to make us lose the identity we have obtained in Christ Jesus.

He will use sin and also attack our natural senses, our mind, our eyes, our ears. He will use any weakness we have, no matter how small, to make us lose our new life and our new identity that we have obtained by the grace of God.

Let us analyze two important points:

a) The evil one does not want you to have an identity.
b) The evil one wants you to lose your identity.

a) The evil one does not want you to have an identity

Satan will not want a Christian to know and understand God's purpose for their life because that will be part of their identity.

By knowing our calling and God's purpose for our life, we will be able to know and position ourselves with that identity.

Knowing and understanding God's call and purpose for our lives will give us an identity in God.

A man or woman who converts to Christianity and does not know God's purpose for their life will lack identity and feel empty. However, if they come to know God's purpose or call for their life, they will feel complete, have peace, and satisfaction because they know they are doing what God wants them to do. They know they are in the position God wants them to be, in the right place.

"For we are his workmanship, created in Christ Jesus unto good works, which God hath before ordained that we should walk in them."
Ephesians 2:10

If the adversary succeeds in delaying or stalling us in our Christian life so that we do not know God's purpose and do not grow spiritually, we will not have our identity in God. If he manages to delay us from knowing our purpose, we will be confused, insecure, and incomplete, lacking clear direction in our spiritual walk.

Many Christians fail to obtain their identity as children of God, and often it is because Satan is preventing it by using confusion, lack of consecration, or lack of dedication to God. We must not be ignorant of our adversary's schemes because many things remain incomplete in our lives due to his influence in some way.

"Be sober, be vigilant; because your adversary the devil, as a roaring lion, walketh about, seeking whom he may devour:"
1 Peter 5:8

We must understand that the enemy does not want you to have your new identity as a Christian. He will try to delay that achievement in your life, leaving you incomplete.

If we are close to God through His Word (the Bible) and His Holy Spirit, we will become what God wants us to be.

Do not allow the devil to distract you, steal your time of communion with God, and thus prevent you from knowing God's purpose for your life.

b) The evil one wants you to lose your identity

"But I fear, lest by any means, as the serpent beguiled Eve through his subtilty, so your minds should be corrupted from the simplicity that is in Christ."
2 Corinthians 11:3

Adam and Eve lost their identity by being deceived by Satan. He not only wants to prevent you from having your identity as a son or daughter of God, but also, if you already have that identity, he wants to take it away, just as he did with Adam and Eve (Genesis 3).

If Satan managed to make Adam and Eve lose the genuine identity they already had as children of God, he will also want to do the same with us. If we already possess an identity in God, he will want to snatch it away, and he will use any means to achieve his purpose.

With Adam and Eve, he used disobedience to God. Even though they had never had a past life like we had before knowing God, the enemy still managed to make them fall from the grace they were in.

With us, he will not only use disobedience to God and His Word, but he will also use the memories of the experiences of our previous life. He will make us remember so that we backslide and return to the life we had left. That is why the Word of God teaches us:

"18. Remember ye not the former things, neither consider the things of old. 19. Behold, I will do a new thing; now it shall spring forth; shall ye not know it? I will even make a way in the wilderness, and rivers in the desert."
Isaiah 43:18-19

If we lose our identity, we will also lose our faith and likewise can lose the purpose of God in our lives.

In the book of Job (Job, chapters 1 and 2), one of Satan's purposes with Job was to make him feel confused as a consequence of everything he was experiencing, but Job did not have confusion or lack of faith in God. Why? Because Job knew who he was as a child of God. Job knew his position before God. That is why Job worshipped and blessed God.

"20. Then Job arose, and rent his mantle, and shaved his head, and fell down upon the ground, and worshipped, 21. And said, Naked came I out of my mother's womb, and naked shall I return thither: the Lord gave, and the Lord hath taken away; blessed be the name of the Lord."
Job 1:20-21

One of the best weapons that the children of God can have is our identity.

If we know God's purpose for our lives, His calling, and our position as children of God, Satan will not be able to influence, confuse, or deceive us into falling.

Knowing all this, we must be diligent and put in our effort in seeking God's will and our identity as children of God. This way, we will be more strengthened and grounded in our Christian life, and we will not be overcome by the evil one.

"Be sober, be vigilant; because your adversary the devil, as a roaring lion, walketh about, seeking whom he may devour:"
1 Peter 5:8

The devil wants to destroy us, to make us lose everything, but God wants to perfect us and give us a new and better life.

"The thief cometh not, but for to steal, and to kill, and to destroy: I am come that they might have life, and that they might have it more abundantly."
John 10:10

The devil will work hard to take away or prevent us from having an identity as children of God, but God will work to give us a new identity and a new life with a new and better purpose.

Chapter 11
Our identity is a Grace from God

"**8.** *For by grace are ye saved through faith; and that not of yourselves: it is the gift of God: 9. Not of works, lest any man should boast.*"
Ephesians 2:8-9

The salvation that God gives to all who receive Him is a gift from God. But in addition to salvation, God gives us many other things. Among them is a new identity, and this identity is also a grace from God.

A Christian's identity is given by God, by His grace. We just need to accept it and achieve it through our faith, our obedience, and our perseverance in God.

A new identity is something that God wants to give to all His children.

In the book of Acts chapter 9, when we see the conversion of Saul of Tarsus, Paul, we can observe that God transformed his entire life and gave him a new life, a new identity. We can also see the disciples of Jesus, how each of them was transformed and became a new person with a new identity.

Identity is given by God freely. God does not only want to give us physical or spiritual blessings, like salvation, the calling that God has for each of us, or spiritual gifts, but He also wants to give each believer an individual and unique identity.

If we focus too much on material blessings from God and do not take much interest in other areas of our lives, such as God's calling, spiritual gifts, or even our identity, we may waste our time on perishable things and delay, or even fail to achieve, the new life and purpose that God has for our lives.

If we lack clarity, if there is no security, if we do not know who we are, what our position is in the body of Jesus, we will not feel fulfilled but rather incomplete and empty.

Jesus had no possessions in this world, but even though He had no earthly goods in His natural life, He knew what His position was in the heavenly places. He knew His position as the Son of God. The identity He had was not based on the material possessions He had, nor was it based on any important position or rank, but His position as the Son of God and His identity were based on what He knew He was in the eyes of God.

It is very important to achieve our own identity as children of God. We only need to attain it by faith and allow God, through His Word and His Holy Spirit, to do the work and complete the change in us.

"Being confident of this very thing, that he which hath begun a good work in you will perform it until the day of Jesus Christ:" Philippians 1:6

THE BOOK OF IDENTITY

This book was inspired by the Holy Spirit to edify the body of Christ.

www.ingramcontent.com/pod-product-compliance
Lightning Source LLC
LaVergne TN
LVHW041535060526
838200LV00037B/1001